Earn a Free College Degree

Patriotic Payback – the Unsung Military Path

MITCHELL ARNOLD

PREFACE

Do you want to serve your country and earn a free college degree by the time you're in your mid-20's? This book covers everything you need to know about military-sponsored scholarships and life in the military. Topics include: financial entitlements that allow military members to earn a free bachelor's or master's degree, Enlisted life, Officer life, the military service Academies, Reserve Officer Training Corps scholarships, military lifestyle, military perks, special operations, and more. If you are looking for a path to a free college education and are willing to consider joining the military, discover the many options available and the benefits you can take advantage of for a lifetime.

I wrote this book because I thought I fully understood the military education benefit system back when I was a senior in high school and deciding which path to pursue. A few years into my ROTC experience, my brothers both ended up going to the Air Force and Naval Academies, and I learned things through their experiences that I never knew. As I served my time on active duty, I continued to learn more each year about the different education opportunities available, such as how amazing the Post 9/11 G.I. Bill is. Over the years I've had many parents and students ask me about ROTC and military life. There is a lot of information out there, but nothing contains all the education options summarized in one spot with all the intricacies spelled out.

My military service was a great experience and meant so much to me… patriotism, camaraderie, life lessons, skills that transfer to the corporate world, discipline. Even though some days weren't the best, the experiences and memories are outstanding and I wouldn't trade them for anything. Hopefully this book will open the door for some of you to have similar experiences who might not have considered it otherwise.

"I can imagine no more rewarding a career. And any man who may be asked in this century what he did to make his life worthwhile, I think can respond with a great deal of pride and satisfaction: 'I served in the United States Navy.'"

- John F. Kennedy

Earn a Free College Degree

Patriotic Payback – the Unsung Military Path

MITCHELL ARNOLD

CONTENTS

INTRODUCTION

How can I make college work financially? This question arises in many of our lives at some point. 99% of the suggestions you will encounter focus on loans, scholarships and grants. There is, however, another path which is often overlooked – the military. This book is a first-hand account that explores your options for a free education paid by the military, as well as details of what you can expect military life to look like.

If you are already familiar with any of these sections, feel free to skim that portion. This book was written to inform the typical 16-24 year old (as well as their parents), who may have no knowledge of the military, what can be expected if you decide to serve in the military either before or after a free college education.

The majority of this book is written in regards to active duty service (with one section dedicated to the Reserves and National Guard). Since my military experience was in the Air Force, some of the content is specific to the Air Force and noted as such. The other branches usually operate very similarly, and sometimes exactly the same way. This book will equip you with an overview of many different subjects to help you make an educated decision about your future.

About Me

I graduated debt-free from a four-year private university which cost upwards of $200,000 using one of the paths identified in this book. I recently separated from my short four-year active duty service commitment as a Captain in the U.S. Air Force. Thanks to the opportunities opened to me by the military, I have been fortunate to be able to save well during my time in the Air Force and enjoy the feeling of financial peace today. If you start in high school, you could be in the same exact position as I am at age 26 after only four years of active duty service. I have lived very comfortably while on active duty, going on fun trips almost monthly and enjoying approximately 600 days off work when combining weekends, federal holidays, vacation days, and military 'family days.' When I satisfied my four-year commitment, I could have continued to serve in the Air Force while enjoying a comfortable and stable lifestyle, but instead chose to move on to a new job in the civilian world. You can follow in my footsteps and do it even better, because I made mistakes along the way and now know the intricacies of how the system works. My two younger brothers went to the Naval Academy and the Air Force Academy, and gave me first-hand insight into their college experiences. I have supervised Enlisted airmen who used the different paths explained in this book to get their Bachelor's and Master's degrees either during their active duty careers or shortly after separating. In addition, several of my Air Force friends commissioned through Officer Training School and have shared their experiences with me.

This book covers all of the options available to you, and includes a lot of information you can't find online even if you knew what to look for. I have presented content from this book in front of groups on several occasions and have fielded many questions about these topics over the years. To help you and equip you for a comfortable and stable future, I've condensed it all into this single book.

What You Learn from the Military

Military service is an outstanding experience, no matter how long you decide to stay on active duty. You will see our nation's defense-force firsthand and learn about our impressive and vast capabilities. You'll be part of a large organization with many different missions and get to work for the greater good of our country. You'll get a new perspective of the world by living in new places and being immersed in organizations with members who come from all walks of life. You'll become disciplined and learn how to be timely, organized, and efficient. You'll have a stable job with the opportunity for future career growth and a nice retirement package if you stay in for the full 20 years.

You can expect the military to invest heavily in you, as they believe their greatest asset is their people. I was continually impressed with the effort they make to develop their people into the best version of themselves. The promotion process values what you do outside the job nearly as much as what you do on the job. You can't just show up and perform well and expect to make it all the way to Chief. You also have to volunteer, fill leadership positions, educate yourself, accomplish training, and make an effort to improve your unit beyond what the basic job duties entail. You have to be a team player. If you're sick or have a family emergency, the military will do its best to take care of you. They will continue to educate and train you over the years so that you evolve into the best version of yourself; one that makes an impact in your unit, community and country.

PART 1

THE ENLISTED
PATH

There are two paths you can choose from in the military: Officer and Enlisted. Without going into too much detail yet, you can join the Enlisted ranks without a bachelor's degree and begin training as soon as there is a job available to be taken. The other option is to earn a bachelor's degree and go through Officer training, which will allow you to commission as a military Officer. The jobs and lifestyles of each are a little different as described below. The Enlisted force makes up about 80% of the total force structure and specializes in the technical work. They are the backbone of our military and propel our nation's military defense.

Note: In my career field, many of our Enlisted already have their bachelor's degree and several even have their master's degree. Don't expect the Enlisted force to be full of people without degrees, because a large percent have them and that percent is growing every year.

How to Enlist

This very day, you could make a visit to what is called a 'recruiter' for any branch of the military and discuss what jobs are available either right now or in the near future that you could fill. Recruiters are military members whose current assignment (which typically lasts about three years in this case) is to work in a geographically-dedicated office and sign people up for their branch of service. The 'recruits' live within the recruiter's region of the United States. There are thousands of recruiting offices nationwide serving the various branches of the military. After speaking with a recruiter, you'll set up an appointment to visit a MEPS (Military Entrance Processing Station) to complete the process.

The MEPS will determine your physical qualifications, aptitude and moral standards. One of the important tests they administer is called the ASVAB (Armed Services Vocational Aptitude Battery). It is a multiple-choice test that helps determine what areas you are strongest in and consequently which careers would fit you best. You will also have a physical examination, which includes height and weight measurements, urine and blood tests, drug and alcohol tests, hearing and vision examinations, etc. The military is interested in recruits who are 'fit to fight,' so they don't accept people who are in poor health or who have various physical limitations. They also don't want to take a chance on someone with certain past criminal issues. If you are in relatively good health and do not have a bad criminal record, you are probably a good candidate to apply. There are exceptions to a lot of issues, so even if you're unsure about your eligibility, it never hurts to ask.

These recruiters have quotas they must meet, interspersed across many different jobs, which are passed down to them from their commands and which they must fill to successfully complete their job. The 'needs of the Air Force/Army/Navy/Marines/Coast Guard' is the top priority and a main factor in what is available and what jobs need to be filled first. Other factors which contribute to your career selection include job availability in fields which aren't as high priority, your ASVAB score (and which areas you tested strongly in), physical requirements (which may be different for each job), and recruit preference for certain career fields.

In regards to the needs of a service, if the Air Force decides it needs 1,000 new airmen to join the Intelligence career field by the end of the year and it is a high priority, that number is broken down to a certain amount in each geographic region based on its population. The recruiters then have to find a way to sign up that many new members to become Intel airmen. If you were to go talk to a recruiter while this quota was active and you tested within that career field's specifications, they would probably tell you they have a spot for you in the Intelligence career field.

What an Enlistment Entails

Typically once you and a recruiter have found a good career field match, you sign a four-year or six-year commitment. This means you will belong to that branch of service for that amount of time, and they can move you anywhere in the world and even transfer you to other jobs if they decide to (this is unusual since they will spend money and time training you to work under the job you sign up for). Under normal circumstances, you do not have the option of ending this commitment early. If you stop showing up, you are considered AWOL (absent without leave) and can be arrested by the military and punished. Do not join the military expecting the option to back out if it isn't for you. All of the perks we will discuss come at the expense of trading personal preferences and certain freedoms for employment, stability, and the ability to earn a college degree at the Government's expense. It isn't for everyone, but I do think anyone who is deemed eligible can be successful in the military with the right mindset and work ethic.

Basic Training

After you sign your commitment and receive your 'orders' (which tell you where to go and when to go there), you'll begin your military career. Enlisted careers begin with basic training. In the Air Force, basic training is held in San Antonio, Texas and lasts approximately eight weeks. Basic training will teach you a broad variety of subjects, including military customs and courtesies, military history, how to march, how to properly wear your uniform, how to work as a team, etc. One objective of basic training is to break you down and force you to team up with your unit in order to achieve desired goals and grow as a team. The military places a lot of emphasis on putting the team and the mission before yourself as an individual. You will take part in physically strenuous activities, you will be yelled at, and the whole time you will be evaluated to see how you respond. You can expect basic training to be challenging but not overwhelming. During basic training, you will live in dorm-style rooms on a military base and will follow a very strict schedule. Expect early wakeups, long days filled with activities, little free time, and nights where you sleep like a baby before waking up and doing it all over again. You might even be lucky enough to be awakened by an air horn every morning. Training is very challenging and feels painful in the moment, but makes for good stories and memories afterwards. Make the most of it and expect to fail many times as you learn in the process.

Technical School

After basic training, you will move to the location of your 'technical school' where you will be taught how to do your specific job. Basic training covers broad military topics, and technical or 'tech' school covers the specifics of how to do your day-to-day job. Tech school length and location depends on your career field and can range from four weeks to six or more months. Tech school is usually a combination of classroom and hands-on learning, so the good news is no more getting yelled at and forced to do hundreds of pushups. After you have completed your tech school, you will then move (called a PCS – permanent change of station) to your first duty station. If you separate after your four-year commitment, this will most likely be your only assignment. It could involve a deployment overseas for a temporary period of time such as six months (sometimes up to a year). If you were to stay in the military longer, you could get a new assignment at a different military base. The length of assignments on the Enlisted side varies broadly based on career field, seniority, and needs of your branch.

Job Examples

There are thousands of jobs on the Enlisted side, and the options vary based on the branch you join. Many jobs you would find in the civilian world have some sort of military spinoff version, and there are obviously plenty of military specialty jobs that do not exist in the civilian side as well. Some jobs on the Enlisted side include optometry, paralegal, pararescue, construction, personnel, photojournalist, pharmacy technician, band, public health, radar, weather systems, aircraft maintenance, aircraft refuelers, radio frequency transmissions, remotely piloted aircraft pilot or maintainer, scientific applications, security forces, space systems operations, signals intelligence, special missions, navigation, special reconnaissance, surgical service, tactical air control party specialist, traffic management, vehicle management, water and fuel systems, operations intelligence, nuclear weapons, munitions systems, electronic maintenance, infantry soldiers, contract specialists, finance…. the list goes on and on. There are tons of options, so you have a good chance of finding at least a few career fields you are interested in. Once in a career field, you may have the option of switching over to a different career field at some point. That depends on the needs of your branch and the needs of your career field. If you were to switch jobs, you would go to the technical school for your new job and then PCS to your new assignment.

Enlisted Active Duty Lifestyle

Once at your first duty station, you will be given some sort of schedule and expectations on your workload. You will have a supervisor who will be senior to you and should act as a mentor and develop you. They are the first person you can turn to when you have questions about your workload, promotions, and the work environment. Eventually you will promote to a higher rank and take on more responsibility. Many schedules are similar to a typical Monday through Friday 8-5 job, but some jobs have shift work with various days and changing hours, some involve night shifts, and some involve 12-hour shifts. Military members are similar to salaried employees – you will not be paid hourly. Technically you are considered 'on call/active' 24/7. Most jobs will not overwork you, but do not expect only a 40-hour work week year-round. Your duty hours could vary greatly based on your career field, and even the career fields with standard work hours sometimes have busy times of the year where you will be expected to work much longer hours. Do your research before signing up for a career field so you can know whether it is the right match for you. Talk to people who are already in that career field and see what they think of it, and what they would do if they were in your shoes. The recruiters are primarily interested in filling their slots so don't assume they're always telling you the whole truth.

Promotions

Many of the lower Enlisted ranks have promotions that are based on the amount of time you have served, with the possibility of promoting earlier than you normally would if you are a standout performer. Once you get through the first few ranks, promotions will get more competitive and your years of experience (time-in-grade) will only make up a portion of your promotion package. The rest will be dependent on how you have risen above your peers. With promotions, your branch of the military will determine a specific amount of troops they want to promote to a rank that year or that promotion cycle. Your promotion package consists of 'bullets' (which are condensed sentences full of military jargon/terminology) that explain your achievements during the previous period. The promotion package also contains your test scores for what is essentially a promotion test. Your package will be graded and stacked up against all the other people who are your rank and who are also competing for a promotion. If, for example, the Air Force wanted to promote 5,000 airmen to Technical Sergeant one period and there are 10,000 airmen who are trying to promote, the top 50% earn the promotion and the other 50% are told "better luck next time" and can compete again the next cycle.

As you work your way upward through the ranks, you will get the chance to lead other Enlisted members in the NCO (Non-Commissioned Officer) & SNCO (Senior Non-Commissioned Officer) ranks. You will also have the opportunity to take on career-broadening jobs and leadership jobs that are not as technically oriented as those of your early years. Everyone pays their dues by doing the grunt work at the lower levels, and the best leaders and most motivated troops can promote to leadership positions to lead the next generation.

Housing

As a single junior Enlisted member, there is a good chance you will live in dorms for your first several years of military life. Instead of receiving cash each month for your housing allowance and food allowance (BAH – Basic Allowance for Housing & BAS – Basic Allowance for Subsistence), you will have a free dorm to live in and receive some sort of meal plan for the base dining facility. For many of the junior Enlisted personnel, whose ages usually range from 18-22, this is somewhat similar to the dorm-style living you might experience in college. Instead of going to class, you go to work. After you have reached a certain level of seniority, or if you are married, you'll have the option of moving out of the dorms and living either off-base wherever you want or in an on-base house or townhome. Base housing availability varies depending on rank and the layout and capacity level of your base. Typically if you live in base-housing, you get to stay in nicer or larger houses as you move up in rank. No matter the size, you do not have to pay for it but also do not receive any BAH payments in your monthly pay. If you were to live off-base instead, you could use your BAH to pay for some of your rent or mortgage and pocket the rest or use it all and pay out of pocket for the remainder. BAH rates vary based on your rank and the city you live in. It is significantly higher in cities with a high cost of living, such as San Francisco or Boston.

Permanent Change of Station (PCS)

Any time you PCS to a new duty station, you will have a brief period of time to get situated in your new city before starting work. If you are a junior Enlisted member and are living in the dorms, you may not receive this since you already have your housing set up. If you will not be living in the dorms, your Commander has the authority to give you up to 10 days of time off to 'house hunt' and find a place to live. The Air Force will also pay for you and your family to stay on-base for up to 10 days in either a hotel or a temporary living facility (TLF) which is usually an on-base apartment or townhome. The other branches have similar policies in place, but the timelines may be a bit different.

One nice perk of the military is that each time you PCS to a new location, the military will pay movers to pack up all your stuff, drive it to your new location, and unpack it all for you. The military will also pay you to transport some of or all of your belongings if it is cheaper than it would cost them to pay a private company. If it would cost the Air Force $1000 to pay a private moving company to move your things, for example, you would receive roughly 95% -- or $950 – to move it yourself. And any time you travel, whether it is for a PCS or a Temporary

Duty Assignment (TDY), you can expect a daily per-diem allotment to cover your food expenses. In addition, there is a monetary allowance to cover gas and wear-and-tear on your car (called 'mileage').

Base Amenities

Military bases are like their own little cities. Besides offices and buildings to store military equipment, many also have a grocery store, base exchange (like a Walmart), gas station, gym/workout facility, dining facility (similar to a high school cafeteria), childcare center, dorms and houses, barber shop, food court (with commercial restaurants), bowling alley, fast food restaurant, event center, chapel, hospital, dental clinic, automotive repair center, education center, family life center, and sometimes even a golf course. Most of them offer discounted rates on the products or services provided.

Degree Options for Enlisted

If you follow the Enlisted path, you have two main options for earning a bachelor's degree. Option one is to take online classes or night classes while you're working full-time on active duty and use the military's tuition assistance program. Option two is to finish your active duty service commitment and then use what's called the Post 9/11 G.I. Bill to pay for your bachelor's degree after you're done with the military.

Online and Night Classes

Under option one, you would work your full-time military job and use the military's Tuition Assistance (TA) program to pay for your online classes or night classes. TA will pay for up to $250 per credit hour, with a maximum of $4,500 per fiscal year. To qualify, you apply for TA and get approval from your supervisor at work. Your supervisor will ensure you are in good standing with your unit and have enough free time to take classes. Sometimes if you are studying for a promotion test or taking an upgrade course or certification course in your career field, your supervisor may want you to wait a few weeks before taking a class. TA is a great option for taking class at one of the local colleges, and many bases have partnerships with local colleges which allow them to teach their classes on-base. There will be GPA requirements for continuing to receive TA for future courses, but there aren't many other stipulations you have to adhere to. You can earn an associate's, bachelor's or even master's degree through this route, or earn a bunch of credit hours to be transferred to a four-year university after you separate.

Post 9/11 G.I. Bill

With option two, you have four years of Post 9/11 G.I. Bill benefits to take advantage of. It is technically considered '36 months' of benefits but does not include the three months of summer each year (so basically September – May for each of four academic years). We'll go into more detail below, but you can choose to be a full-time student at a university while not working at all and still receive a room & board stipend, or you can add a part time job to earn some more money. The other option is to work a full-time civilian job and use the benefits to pay for night/online/weekend classes and pocket the room & board stipend.

The combination of TA and the Post 9/11 G.I. Bill would involve taking classes while still active duty via online/night/weekend options to earn the equivalent of two years of credit towards a bachelor's degree. Then after separating from the military, you can go to a normal four-year university and transfer all of that college credit to your new school so you either finish your bachelor's degree in only two years or don't have to take very many classes for three or four years. You could join the working world quicker if you're only a full-time student for two years, and you could save your other two years of benefits for either a master's degree in the future or to pass on to a spouse or dependent down the road.

Note – the rules on this have recently changed so if you

are going to rely on this option, make sure to research the latest news on the subject first. As of August 2019 they are requiring at least six years of active duty service and agreeing to four more years of active duty service at the time of your transfer request in order to pass it on to a spouse or child.*

On the tuitions side of things, the Post 9/11 G.I. Bill will pay for all of your tuition at a public university. Or, instead, it could pay up to $24,476.79 towards a private school's tuition per academic year in 2019-2020. This number increases each year with inflation and rising tuition costs. Some private schools cost more than this, and there is a way around these higher costs through a program called The Yellow Ribbon. If a school is a Yellow Ribbon school, they have elected to pay for either all or part of the remaining tuition for Post 9/11 G.I. Bill recipients for either all or part of applying eligible students (sometimes determined on a first-come first-served basis and sometimes based on merit). There are databases online that show which schools offer Yellow Ribbon programs and how much financial aid each of the schools offer. Besides tuition, you will also receive up to $1,000 per year for books and study materials.

Note: these numbers are assuming you are considered a full-time student. At many schools this is at least 9 or 12 credit hours. If you are not full-time, you receive a % of the benefit based on how many hours you are taking. There are plenty of articles online with all of the breakdowns.

Separate from tuition and the books stipend in the Post 9/11 G.I. Bill, you will also receive a room and board stipend of approximately $1,400/month. This amount could be much higher since it is adjusted based on the cost of living in your school's city. To see what your allowance would be, go to a military pay table online and look up BAH (Basic Allowance for Housing) for an E5 with dependents in the city of the university you are considering attending. It is the E5 with dependents rate for everyone, no matter what rank you were upon separating. (https://militarybenefits.info/bah-calculator/)

Montgomery G.I. Bill

A third option is the Montgomery G.I. Bill, which is not usually used for a bachelor's degree. This can be used in place of the Post 9/11 G.I. Bill. The Montgomery G.I. Bill is better for those interested in an approved vocational training program (on-the-job training, flight training, apprenticeships, prep courses, etc.) instead of a degree at a typical four-year university. You will receive up to $1,648 per month for 36 months while you are participating in one of these programs. To receive this bill you usually have to contribute about $100 per month for twelve months from your paycheck towards this program when you first begin active duty. You are then considered 'vested' and have the option of using the Montgomery G.I. Bill after you separate.

Enlisted Summary

The easiest and most assured way to get a free college education is to enlist in the military after high school, serve on active duty for four years, separate, and use the Post-9/11 G.I. Bill to pay for your bachelor's degree and living expenses for the next four years. You will spend your time from age 18-22 maturing and learning a new trade while serving your country (and getting paid for it), and you will get to experience a new part of the country and/or the world. After four years, you have the option to separate if you choose and become a civilian again (but with lifetime benefits only available to veterans). Being a freshman in college at age 22 has plenty of perks. You can drink legally if you choose to, you're disciplined enough to not blow off class, and you are a mature and attractive option in the dating field. One of my buddies in my college fraternity was a former Marine and got to experience the best of both worlds. He valued his military experience and the college experience he earned as a result of his service.

PART 2

THE OFFICER PATH

The Officer path is more selective than the Enlisted path, with Officers making up about 20% of the total force structure. While Officers have a job that falls under a specific career field category (Air Force Specialty Code or AFSC in the Air Force), they are primarily considered managers and leaders who can be moved around to different units and missions, and will not specialize in a specific type of work for more than a few assignments. Before becoming an Officer, you must have a Bachelor's degree and complete an Officer training program. Upon completion of these tasks, you will earn your 'commission' and become a Commissioned Officer.

How to Become an Officer

There are three main paths to becoming an Officer: the first is through a Federal Service Academy, to include the Air Force Academy, Naval Academy, Military Academy at West Point, Coast Guard Academy, and Merchant Marine Academy, the second is Reserve Officer Training Corps (ROTC) at a university or non-federal military service academy, and the third is through Officer Training School/Officer Candidate School (OTS/OCS).

There is also an option called a direct-commission but these are rare and are usually reserved for highly selective career fields like doctors and lawyers.

Military members going through Officer training via an Academy, ROTC or OTS/OCS are called 'Cadets' in the Air Force/Army/Coast Guard, but called 'Midshipmen' in the Navy (who can later commission as Naval Officers or

Marine Officers). For the sake of conciseness, all will be referred to as Cadets in the following sections.

Federal Service Academy

To attend a Federal Service Academy, you must go through a highly selective and extensive application process. Besides the normal components of a college application package, you also must receive a senatorial or congressional nomination. The nomination process is lengthy, and each nominating authority has its own processes and deadlines. If you are in high school, it is recommended to begin the process during the spring or summer after your junior year. The most common nominations are Congressional nominations. Each member of Congress is allowed to have up to five cadets attend each Department of Defense (DoD) Academy at one time. For each of the five possible slots that are empty for an upcoming academic year, they are allowed to nominate up to ten candidates who would then all compete for acceptance at their respective Academy. *The Merchant Marine Academy grants 10 slots per member of Congress instead of five, and the Coast Guard Academy does not require a nomination. You should request a nomination from both of your U.S. Senators and your U.S. Representative. These nominations are awarded based on the combination of leadership performance, academic achievement, and athletic participation. Besides Congressional, the other categories of nominations include Presidential, Vice Presidential, Military Affiliated, and U.S. Territory and International categories. These are less common but can be pursued if you qualify.

The Academies have acceptance rates hovering around 10%-15% and are considered highly selective. If you are selected, you leave for basic training the summer after you graduate high school and remain in a military environment almost full-time for the next four years of your life. It is a rigorous but rewarding four years, and not everyone makes it through. Most graduates consider it a great experience. One recent graduate from the Naval Academy said that while part of him wished he had the normal college experience, he made some of the best friends of his life and was able to do lots of cool things that most of the population doesn't ever get the chance to do. He was paid to do it, and also enjoyed the great benefit of graduating completely debt free while enjoying a beautiful campus on the East Coast in Annapolis, Maryland. A recent graduate from the Air Force Academy called it the best experience of his life. He learned a lot and met plenty of awesome people at the Academy. He valued the great exposure to the operational Air Force and the many Officers and mentors that were available to share advice and their experiences. There is also an outstanding network of Academy graduates you will have access to for life after graduation. Air Force Academy cadets get to enjoy their college experience in the beautiful city of Colorado Springs right at the base of the Rocky Mountains. At all military service academies, you will have the opportunity to learn and grow exponentially in your leadership capacity as you train to commission as an Officer.

The Merchant Marine Academy is located in New York, northeast of Queens and close to Manhattan. This is the only Academy that falls under the Department of Transportation. The Military Academy at West Point (Army) is located in New York on the Hudson River. West Point, along with the Air Force Academy and Naval Academy, fall under the Department of Defense. The Coast Guard Academy is located in New London, Connecticut on the Thames River right by the ocean, between New York City and Boston. It is the only federal service academy that does not require a Congressional nomination for admission, and falls under the Department of Homeland Security.

Lifestyle Overview

Academy cadets balance a full academic class schedule semester with other daily and weekly activities specific to the service academies. All cadets must be enrolled in a minimum of 15 semester hours during their entire four-year tenure. The average amount of class taken by cadets is closer to 18-22 hours per semester, but can vary based on which major you pursue and if you choose to have a minor. Academy cadets wear some type of uniform on-campus for the majority of their time there, and don't earn certain privileges like having a car or being allowed off-campus until they've reached a certain seniority level. Cadets are encouraged to take part in some sort of academic, religious, or other extracurricular group in addition to their military obligations, academic classes, and athletic endeavors.

All Federal Service Academies require a 5-year active

duty service commitment upon graduation/commissioning. Certain jobs like pilots, as well as other operational career fields, typically require longer commitments in addition to the time spent training for that job. Air Force pilots owe 10 years plus their training time, regardless of their source of commissioning.

Scholarships & Stipends

One of the best perks of the Academies is that you do not pay a dime out of pocket for basically anything essential, including tuition, room & board, uniforms, haircuts, etc. Additionally, you earn a nice stipend each month. For most of the Academies this monthly stipend is around $1100 per month, but cadets start with a 'debt' to pay for all the gear they are issued such as uniforms and laptops. Part of their monthly stipend is set aside to automatically pay off this debt. Of the leftover money, some is set aside in a fund that accumulates throughout a cadet's time at the Academy and then is paid out as a lump sum during their junior or senior year. The rest of the leftover money is paid to the cadets monthly. At the Naval Academy, midshipmen will see about $100/month, then $200/month, then $400/month their first three years respectively before receiving a large lump sum of around $8,000. Then their senior year they receive the full monthly payouts minus recurring expenses for services such as laundry, barbershop, etc. At the Air Force Academy, cadets see closer to $200/month, $500/month, and $700/month their first three years respectively before the large lump sum payment and then follow-on payments of nearly the full $1,100 per month. The amounts will vary at each Academy based on the costs of uniforms and recurring expenses.

Upon graduation and commissioning, West Point and Naval Academy graduates receive 30 days of paid leave to travel or relax before their specialized training begins while Air Force Academy graduates get 60 days. All receive their full base pay and basic allowance for housing (depending on where their Academy is located).

Service Commitment

Another fantastic perk of the service academies is the fact that you do not owe anything to the military until you sign your commitment in the summer or fall of your junior year of college. That means you could attend for two full years for free and then drop out with no strings attached if it is not the right fit for you. You will not owe any money back and can transfer your college credits to another institution to finish out there. Once you sign the commitment and begin your third year, you are committed to finishing your time there or pay the hefty price tag for tuition reimbursement and possibly Enlisted service.

Physical Training

All of the Academies place a big emphasis on athletics. Most of them require Physical Education classes like boxing, unarmed combatives, water survival, swimming, and elective sports. The Naval Academy has a sports period every day, where everyone is encouraged to go out and do something physical. Nearly everyone is either on an intercollegiate athletics sports team (varsity or club) or an intramural team. One of their slogans is "Everyone is an athlete." At the Air Force Academy, they have training sessions in the afternoons to do a mandatory physical activity, such as intramurals or intercollegiate athletics. Depending on your unit, you may participate in workouts as a group. Your Commander and leadership team has the option of requiring them, but they are not very common unless dealt as a punishment or part of a training weekend. Freshmen at any of the Academies can expect to perform a lot of PT activities.

Academic Classes

Just like any college or university, the Academies have a variety of majors to choose from in a variety of fields. There is a base curriculum which all students must complete, and there is also a major-specific curriculum. Additionally, the Academies require at least one or two military classes each semester that you wouldn't find at a typical university. At the Naval Academy, these included courses over seamanship and navigation, leadership principles, naval weapon systems, and naval history. The Air Force Academy has curriculum on military strategic studies, military training, and Officer-development leadership courses.

Summer Programs

Summers are typically broken up into three blocks at the Academies, each lasting about a month. One block is set aside for leave/vacation, and the other two are different each year and depend on your interests after graduation. At the Naval Academy, one block is typically designated for some sort of professional development training while the other is known as a Fleet Cruise. These two blocks consist of a wide variety of career experiences at nearly any geographical location around the world.

The professional training has options such as: being a Northern Tier or Philmont guide if you were ever involved in Boy Scouts, outdoor backpacking experiences designed to build teamwork and leadership skills (called NOLS and Rocky Mountain High), internships through many esteemed private corporations or collegiate research programs, and summer study abroad programs in foreign countries. Being an Information Technology major, my brother did two separate internships with the NSA.

The Fleet Cruise block changes for each of your three summers after basic training. Going into your sophomore year, you will be stationed on a ship or submarine for a month and paired with an Enlisted sailor who you will shadow for the entirety of the cruise. This gives you an appreciation for what life is like from the Enlisted perspective, along with teaching you how the fleet operates on a daily basis. The following summer you will partake in Protramid (similar to Cortramid in ROTC programs) which gives you one week of experience in each of the

Navy's four central communities; surface, submarine, aviation, and marine. The final summer's fleet cruise is up to you. Since you will be making your career selection the following summer, Midshipmen typically choose to spend that block with whatever community they intend to join after graduation. For example, if you were interested in the Marine Corps, you could do "Leatherneck" at Quantico, VA where new Marine Officers train. If you wanted to be a pilot, you could do an "Aviation Cruise" with a fleet squadron where you would get the chance to go on flights and experience the lifestyle of an active duty aviation unit.

At the Air Force Academy, the options are flexible. The summer after freshman year, most cadets participate in survival training and an airmanship program, such as sky diving, flying gliders, or operating space/drone assets. The next summer, cadets participate in one leadership program, such as leading Basic Cadet Training or leading an airmanship program. A common summer segment is called 'Ops Air Force' where cadets visit an operational Air Force base somewhere in the world and gain experience with a real, operational Squadron. Other options include traveling to other countries for language development and/or cultural immersion (such as visiting Spain for a Spanish language minor) or taking summer academic classes. The summer before Senior year requires two blocks of leadership. This could be a combination of leadership and some other required courses. Another popular option at this level is called the Cadet Summer Research Program (CSRP), allowing cadets to work an internship in private industry based on your academic major. These are typically 5-week programs with a company or an organization in the Air Force or Department of Defense.

Graduate School Options

The Academies offer a larger and better selection of graduate school opportunities upon graduation. At the Air Force Academy, there are three tiers of opportunities depending on your GPA. They start screening for who they project will be the most qualified during sophomore year. The first tier is for international programs such as the Rhodes, Gates-Cambridge, Truman, and Schwarzman scholarships. The second tier is through nationally competitive scholarships with programs like MIT, Rice, Stanford, Purdue, Washington, and Harvard. For this tier you will compete against non-Air Force Academy students, but the AFA has a good relationship with these schools so there is a good chance you can get selected. The third tier is through the Graduate Studies Program (GSP). Every academic major is allocated an amount of funding from the Air Force Institute of Technology to send some of their graduates in that major to pursue a Master's degree at any University that fits within that budget. There is an assumption that if you are selected for the GSP scholarship, you will come back as an instructor for that department later in your military career. If the Air Force Institute of Technology offers a Master's degree in your field of study, you could go straight to AFIT instead (located at Wright Patterson AFB,

Ohio). Certain jobs in the Air Force require a Master's degree before you begin your first assignment, such as the Operations Research Analyst career field. The other Academies also have a vetting process similar to the Air Force's (such as the Trident Scholars Program at the Naval Academy). If you aren't selected for a graduate degree immediately after commissioning, you may still have the option of pursing one as a future assignment based on your career field.

Reserve Officer Training Corps

Lifestyle Overview

Reserve Officer Training Corps (ROTC) is a mixture of military life with college life. This was the path that I took. While a ROTC cadet, I lived like a typical college student except for two hours on Tuesdays and four hours on Thursdays. We had PT (physical training) twice per week for one hour each day. We had one military-related academic class per week – a one credit hour class as a freshman and sophomore, and a three credit hour class as a junior and senior. Leadership laboratory (or Lead Lab as we called it) was two hours long but counted as one credit hour. It took place once per week in one long session (on Thursday afternoons for us). Almost all other ROTC-related events were encouraged but voluntary. These included activities such as visits to nearby bases, sporting events with other ROTC organizations, mock field training, and professional development sessions. My detachment required us to wear uniforms all day on Tuesday and Thursday while we were on-campus, which included going to non-ROTC classes and the cafeteria. Many detachments only require uniforms for one day per week, and some detachments only require them while doing ROTC activities. If you're curious how your ROTC detachment operates at the school you're interested in, reach out to them and ask if you can talk to them on the phone to get a better idea of their policies. They are happy to answer questions and want to bring in as many new prospects as possible.

Unlike the Academies which require a five-year active

duty commitment upon graduation, ROTC graduates only require a four-year service commitment. However, you may have to wait several months or even up to a year after graduation to begin your time, whereas the Academies begin right at graduation. If you get matched with a certain job like pilot and other operational career fields, you will still incur longer service commitments in addition to the training period. This is because the training associated with these jobs is expensive for the military to provide to you, and they want to get back an appropriate return on their investment.

Scholarships & Stipends

Type 1 Air Force ROTC (AFROTC) scholarships cover 100% of tuition no matter where you go, whether a public school or private school. These scholarships only make up about 5-10% of the AFROTC four-year scholarships given out, and nearly all of them are awarded with the requirement of earning a technical degree (such as electrical, mechanical, or aeronautical engineering). Type 2 AFROTC scholarship cover a certain amount of tuition, currently $18,000, and make up about 20% of all scholarships given out. This will cover tuition at most public universities, and a decent chunk of tuition at many private universities. Type- 7 AFROTC scholarships cover 100% of tuition at a public institution (not at a private institution) with an AFROTC detachment. These are the majority of scholarships they give out. The current deadline for high school AFROTC scholarship applications is January 17, 2020. More information can be found at https://www.afrotc.com/scholarships/.

Apart from the four-year scholarships available to high school students, you can also earn a variety of ROTC scholarships once you are already in college. Many of these will start the semester after you are selected and last for the remainder of your college career. The two main classifications are similar to the high school types above: Type 1 are more selective (and only for technical majors) and cover full tuition at any public or private university, and Type 2 pay up to $18,000 per year in tuition. Both also come with a monthly stipend and book stipend. Keep in mind that these in-college scholarships are selective and each detachment is only able to give out a limited amount.

The annual book stipend is $900 per academic year ($450 per semester), and the monthly stipend – which can be spent on whatever you want – increases as a student completes each year of college. Freshmen receive $300 per month, sophomores receive $350 per month, juniors receive $450 per month, and seniors receive $500 per month. As a college student, I mainly used this on Chipotle and beer (don't tell my mom). There are 145 Air Force ROTC detachments, and these detachments play host to over 1,100 associated cross-town universities.

There are a variety of Army ROTC scholarships which include two-year, three-year, and four-year scholarships. All of them pay full tuition and fees, and include a book stipend and a monthly stipend. There are 273 Army ROTC programs spread across the United States.

There are 63 Navy ROTC units hosted at 77 schools throughout the nation, and the program is available at over 160 colleges and universities through either the host school or through a cross-town enrollment agreement. Similar to Army ROTC, Navy ROTC also offers full tuition and other financial benefits for books and education fees. There is no Marine ROTC, but graduates of Navy ROTC programs may commission as either Marine Officers or Navy Officers since the Marine Corps is a branch of the Department of the Navy. The Coast Guard does not have an ROTC program.

Service Commitment

Joining your local ROTC detachment does not incur any kind of service commitment right away, and neither does accepting a high school ROTC scholarship. If you are a scholarship cadet, you can go through your entire freshman year of college and then opt out before starting your sophomore year without any penalties. None of the scholarship money you received will be owed back to the military and no service commitment will be owed back either. You sign your service commitment in your sophomore year and then you are in.

If you are not a scholarship cadet, you can go through your first two years of ROTC before signing your service commitment at the beginning of your junior year. And a side note for these cadets – if you were not on scholarship while in ROTC, you can begin to earn Post 9/11 G.I. Bill eligibility right when you begin active duty instead of having to pay off your service commitment first like the scholarship cadets.

Physical Training

Physical Training (PT) is a staple at all ROTC programs. The time and duration of PT depends on your ROTC program; our detachment held PT at 5pm on Tuesdays and 6pm on Thursdays, but many are in the mornings. Ours was so late in the day because our detachment was a host detachment and nearby satellite schools came to our detachment to take part in our program. It would have required uncomfortably early travel to get people who live an hour away to show up for a 6am workout. PT is usually a combination of cardio, calisthenics, and sports. Some detachments may play a sport once every week or two, and others may only play sports a few times per semester. As a cadet, you will typically take the Physical Fitness Assessment/Test (PFA/PFT) at least once per semester and sometimes more often. The PFA for the Air Force consists of a 1.5 mile run, one minute of as many pushups as you can do, one minute of as many sit-ups as you can do, a waist circumference measurement and a height/weight measurement. There are minimums for each category that you must achieve to pass, and you score higher based on how well you perform in each area. The Army, Marines, and Navy each have a different physical fitness test, and all of them are a bit tougher than that of the Air Force. Military members are expected to be physically fit at all times (often termed 'fit to fight').

Many people will try to get in shape right before the test, but the correct approach is to always be in good enough shape to pass the test. Failure of a fitness test as a scholarship ROTC cadet can result in the loss of your scholarship, and failure as a Commissioned Officer can result in you being kicked out of the military (discharged); it is not something to mess around with.

Academic Classes

For Air Force ROTC, we had what were called AS Classes (Air Sciences classes) which was the military academic curriculum broken into four years worth of classes. The AS 100 freshman level class is a one-hour class and focuses on the Foundations of the Air Force. The AS 200 class for sophomores is also a one-hour class and focuses on the Evolution of Aerospace Studies. If you were to join ROTC as a sophomore, you could take both classes at once. The AS 300 class is for juniors and is a three-hour class. It is more challenging and focuses on Leadership Studies. The AS 400 class is for seniors and is also a three-hour class which focuses on National Security Studies and Preparation for Active Duty. You will earn a grade in each class that is factored into your school's GPA.

Based on the size of your detachment, there may only be one offering for the day of the week and time to meet. As freshman and sophomores who have many options for the other classes they take, the ROTC detachment will probably expect you to take the timeslot they offer and base the rest of your academic class selection around it. If you're the only one who can't take it due to an impossible conflict with your major, your detachment may let you take the class a year later. If several cadets have scheduling issues, they may offer a second class. As juniors and seniors with less schedule flexibility, your detachment may have all cadets at your level send in availability and then schedule your class for the time that works best for everyone else. Unfortunately for me, my senior year we had to schedule our class at 6am on Friday mornings because that's the only time that worked for everybody. Hopefully you will end up with a much better timeslot.

Leadership Laboratory

Leadership Laboratory – or Lead Lab as we called it – is set up so the juniors and seniors create and administer the training for the freshmen and sophomores. They are tasked with teaching the underclassmen everything they need to know to be successful at Field Training. This is where military activities like marching, customs & courtesies, career fairs, etc. take place. Expect your lead labs to take place as a single two-hour block of time. We also had one mandatory weekend activity per semester for mock field training, which was usually 24 to 36 hours of training at an off-site location. Army ROTC and Navy ROTC have a similar program in place.

Field Training

Field Training is ROTC's equivalent of Basic Training. Earning an invitation to Field Training is a competitive process, and attending Field Training is a competitive and taxing experience. It is a bootcamp style program which includes weapons training, survival training, deployment skills, aircraft indoctrination, teambuilding, physical conditioning, and many other activities. Earning a field training slot is based on a combination of your PT scores, your Detachment Commander's rating of you compared to your peers, and your academic GPA. Cadets on scholarship are not guaranteed a Field Training slot. Field Training usually takes place during the summer between sophomore and junior year. In the Air Force, it is a five-week program that takes place at Maxwell AFB in Alabama for the first half and Camp Shelby in Mississippi for the second half. Note: the program length has changed a few times recently and could vary from four to five weeks based on which summer you attend. Cadets at Field Training should be prepared before arrival, which is different than Enlisted and Academy basic trainings where they show up knowing nothing and learn everything on the fly. Like the other basic trainings, it is filled with marching, group activities, being yelled at, various types of training, and simulations. Graduation from Field Training is required before advancing to ROTC's upper class (POC - Professional Officer Corps). If you don't earn a Field Training slot your first year, you can try again the next year and sometimes the year after that. But you will continue to take part in the 200-level curriculum until you complete Field Training.

A typical day at Air Force Field Training looks like this: 0400 wakeup, 0410 march to PT, 0430-0530 PT, 0540-0600 shower and get dressed, 0610 morning formation, 0630-0700 breakfast, then a combination of academic classes, hands-on training such as combatives, lunch, seminars, more physical training, marching, teambuilding, dinner, and bedtime at 2100. This schedule continues for the entirety of your training.

Non-Federal Military Academies

There are a few non-federal military academies you may have heard of. These include the Citadel, Virginia Military Institute (VMI), and similar programs like the Corps at Texas A&M and Virginia Tech. These schools and programs have some similarities to the federal Academies and some similarities to ROTC. They are all unique in their own ways, but most of them involve a full-time military environment similar to the Academies. However, they technically act as ROTC programs. You can commission as an Officer of any branch of the military out of each of them. They all have their own traditions and loyal alumni networks, and they operate independently of each other.

Officer Training School/Officer Candidate School

OTS/OCS is the third and final main path to becoming an Officer. Depending on which branch you join, it will be called either OTS or OCS but it is essentially the same program. This path consists of earning your bachelor's degree and then filling out an application for OTS/OCS. If you are accepted, you'll be offered a job in the branch you applied for, and if you take it, you'll go through a condensed Officer training and then head to your first assignment. In the Air Force, the training is a three-month course at Maxwell AFB in Alabama. After graduating from OTS, you commission and begin active duty just like everyone else. This path leads to the same result if successful, but being accepted will depend on the needs of your branch of service at the time, as well as the jobs they are trying to fill. If you have a specific job that you really want, this may not be the best path for you. The Academies typically get a broad selection of career fields to choose from. The top ROTC graduates may get what they want but the rest may not have as broad of a career field selection as the Academies. OTS gets its own allotment and it is not quite the same as either of the first two commissioning paths. A nice perk of OTS is they are offered their career field before they sign their contract and before attending training, whereas ROTC and Academy cadets don't find out until their senior year. Both get to put in their job preferences, but it then becomes a matching game where those who are rated the highest get first dibs on what they want and everything else trickles down to those rated below them.

Commissioning

No matter what path you take, after you have completed it you will commission as a 2nd Lieutenant in the Air Force, Army and Marines (Navy has different terms for their Officer ranks; they begin as an Ensign). Some argue that the

Academies do the best job of preparing their Officers for life on active duty, but many believe ROTC and OTS do a more than adequate job of preparation for active duty. The major tangible difference between the programs is the job options which will be available to you before you commission. While ROTC cadets can become pilots, there are a higher percentage of pilot slots set aside for Academy graduates. As you become more senior in rank over time, having a degree from an Academy could help you get promoted to some of the highest ranks in the military. However, there are plenty of ROTC graduates who have been extremely successful in their military careers and who have made four-star General ranks.

Note: Officers who commission through ROTC may have to wait up to one year after commissioning before beginning active duty. This is entirely dependent on your assignment and the needs of your branch. You can use this time to travel, relax, or work a different job. Once you start active duty, half of the time you had to wait is counted towards your promotion dates so you will promote a bit faster than the two year wait that is normal for company grade Officers (O1 – O3, the first three paygrades/ranks for the Officer Corps).

Officer Tuition Assistance & G.I. Bill

Officers may use TA towards a master's degree while active duty. It pays up to $250 per semester credit hour and cannot exceed $4,500 per fiscal year. Something to keep in mind that the Enlisted don't have to worry about is that Officers must fulfill a service obligation that runs parallel with, but not in addition to, their existing service obligation. For the Air Force it is two years, so if I'm a 2nd Lt in the Air Force and have three years left of service obligation, I can use TA without adding onto my commitment. But if I am a year from separating and use TA, I will have to extend my service obligation by one year.

Officers can earn the Post 9/11 or Montgomery G.I. Bill, but first they have to work off their time owed from either their Academy service commitment or ROTC scholarship commitment. For me personally, I owed four years of service for my four-year ROTC scholarship. I would not start earning Post 9/11 G.I. Bill eligibility until I had served for a full four years. In order to earn full eligibility you need to serve three years, so I would have earned 100% eligibility if I had served for seven years. OTS graduates start earning GI Bill eligibility immediately since they did not receive any scholarship for their college degree.

Note: More information about the Post 9/11 G.I. Bill is located in a section above under 'Degree Options for Enlisted'

Officer Pay

You can expect your starting pay to be about $4,000 per month after taxes if you're stationed in the Midwest or the South, and considerably higher if you're in a more urban area on the east or west coast. When you promote to O2 after two years (1st Lieutenant in the Marines/Army/AF), your base pay will increase over 30% and your housing allowance will increase a couple hundred dollars. After you've been an O2 for a year, your base pay will bump up roughly another 17%. When you promote to O3 a year after that, it will jump another 17% and your housing allowance will increase again. You will end up with your base pay about 78% higher than when you first started four years prior, as well as a higher housing allowance.

Officer Housing

Officers are not expected or given the option to stay in dorms when they first start active duty. You will have the option of either living on-base in a house or townhome, or living off-base wherever you want. If you live on-base, you will not receive your housing allowance (BAH) but you will not have to pay rent and sometimes you won't even have to pay for your utilities. If you live off-base, you will receive your housing allowance and can pocket what you don't spend of it, or use some of your base pay if you spend more than it covers. On-base housing is subject to availability and will depend on your rank and the base you are stationed at. From my experience, it seems to make the most sense to live on-base if you have a family or if you are working long hours and do not have much free time. If you are single and working regular hours, it may be more fun to live off-base.

Note: while you are completing training for your career field (tech school) before your first assignment, you may be required to stay on-base in dorm-style or apartment-style housing. This is temporary and the training courses usually last no longer than 6 months to a year.

Some Officers choose to purchase a home at each

new duty station they move to, and when they move to their next assignment they lease out their home. While there can be headaches associated with leasing out a property, there are long-term financial benefits to doing this. Owning homes near military bases means there will always be a demand for housing, and renting to military families can alleviate some of the pains of leasing out your property since you know the character of the average military member. You also know they have a Commander who you can contact if they aren't paying their rent. As you continue to add to your property portfolio over time, and if each of their mortgages are being paid off by the people you are leasing to, you can end up with outright ownership on many valuable properties by your 50's or 60's. Then you can sell most of them and add that cash to your retirement fund, or buy a nice big house outright and use your military retirement pay to cover your living expenses.

Officer Jobs

Many jobs fall into an encompassing category, and the different branches have different terms for them but they are all similar. Let's use the Air Force's for example. In the Air Force, a Wing (an entity with a specific mission) is located at a base (or sometimes several bases) and is broken into several Groups. One or two Groups will run the operational mission. For the Air Force, this could include an Ops Group that is in charge of a flying mission or a flight training mission. It could also include a Cyber Security Group which is in charge of either cyber-attacks or cyber defense of our systems. Supporting that operational group(s) is a Mission Support Group made up of different components that facilitate the successful completion of that mission. At my base, our Mission Support Group was made up of a Logistics Readiness Squadron that transported and ordered cargo and necessary supplies, a Force Support Squadron that took care of the assignments and paperwork for all troops on base and ran base facilities (like the gym, hotel, dining facility, etc.), a Contracting Squadron who wrote contracts for and purchased all the goods and services used on base (grounds maintenance, janitorial services, desks, computers, building construction/repair, etc.), a Security Forces Squadron in charge of defending the base (similar to the police), and finally the Civil Engineering Squadron that was in charge of managing all the construction projects on base and keeping everything in working order. There was also a Medical Group in charge of keeping everyone healthy. They ran what is essentially the base hospital, and have various sections for different aspects of health. Officer jobs in the medical career field include doctors, dentists, nurses, aides, etc.

Some careers like doctors offer a direct-commissioning program and they begin as high- ranking Officers depending on their career field. This is to help decrease the difference in pay when compared to the private sector.

Officer Active Duty Lifestyle

Due to the enormous variety of Officer jobs in the military, it is difficult to encompass all of them in this section. A few things you can expect regardless of career field, though, include the following: you will have an extremely stable job with reasonable working hours and great benefits, you will be developed by your branch of the military to become the best version of yourself that you can be, you will be treated with respect by your peers (whether Officer, Enlisted, or Civilian), you will have a degree of flexibility in selecting follow-on assignments if you choose to stay in the service, and finally, each assignment will take you to a new part of the world and will be unique from past assignments. I encourage you to find someone who is an active duty Officer in the career field you are interested in and ask them what their lifestyle is like to get a better idea of what to expect.

Career Broadening Assignments

The military tries to develop Officers into well-rounded leaders. This means they can't just be experienced in their own career field, but also need experience from other career fields as well. If you were an Acquisitions Officer for example, a good match for a career broadening assignment might be in the logistics field. There are joint-assignments where you will work at another branch's base or headquarters and see firsthand how the culture is different and how the different branches work together to achieve the mission. Another career broadening assignment could be as an instructor for pilot training, or as a professor at a military service academy or ROTC detachment, or even doing a completely different job than you are used to. Though it isn't considered career broadening, you will probably also have to work as an executive Officer at some point if you stay in the military. This encompasses being the aide to a high-ranking Officer and setting his/her schedule, preparing and routing documents and assignments for completion and signature, etc. It may not be very fun and typically requires long hours, but you learn a lot from a mentor who has been successful in their career and who can show you the dedication it takes to be a high-ranking leader.

PART 3

MILITARY INFO NUGGETS

Differences of each Branch

Each of the five branches of the military have different histories and missions, as well as very different cultures and attitudes. The Air Force focuses on its mission which is split between air, space, and cyber power. Since the other branches also have air components, there are talks of a shift to more of a cyber and space focus for the Air Force in the future. The operations side of the Air Force still includes a heavy lean towards missions with fighter jets, bombers, refuelers, and cargo transportation. Air Force bases are located all over the world and typically have nice facilities because they receive large financial budgets to cover their expensive air mission. The Air Force used to be part of the Army (at the time, they were called the Army Air Corps) before breaking off and becoming an independent branch in 1947.

The Army is the oldest branch of the military, and its culture is similar to what most think of when they think of the military. They are the largest branch and have many old traditions. Like the Air Force and Navy, the Army has bases that are located all over the U.S.

The Marines pride themselves on their ability to support all the different components of an attack by themselves. They navigate on the water or through the air to a location, drop ground troops and complete their task without support from the other branches. The Marines fall under the Department of the Navy and fly fighter jets and helicopters. They adhere strictly to military tradition and customs &

courtesies.

The Navy is almost as old as the Army. They have many rich traditions and embrace the sailor persona. The Navy has many bases in beautiful locations along both coasts in the continental United States, as well as on the water in many gorgeous international locations. The Navy does have a flying mission but its main mission is sea focused. Their vehicles include boats, ships, submarines, fighter jets, and large planes that can find and take down underwater vessels (called Maritime Patrol aircraft). Though it may vary based on your job, joining the Navy means there's a good chance you'll spend a lot of time out on the ocean on a boat or sub.

The Coast Guard is no longer part of the Department of Defense like the other four branches; they now fall under the Department of Homeland Security. The Coast Guard may get a slightly bad rap because they aren't on the offensive side of things, but they defend our home soil and have lots of interesting missions. A large one that many people are familiar with is the drug wars with organizations from other countries who try to sneak large shipments of drugs onto our soil. They also have search and rescue missions for boats that get lost or sink off our shores. The Coast Guard has many bases in beautiful locations in the United States along the coasts.

Special Operations

Many high schoolers are interested in a Special Ops job, such as Navy SEAL, Army Rangers, or Air

Force PJ's. This section covers a brief overview of what you can expect based on my interviews with current special ops members and candidates. It focuses on the Navy SEAL (acronym for SEa, Air, Land) process, but the Army Rangers and Air Force PJ's have similar processes in place.

If you want to enlist as a Special Operations member in the Navy, you will sign your service commitment contract as a special ops member. It is selective to get assigned with this job in the first place, and then the actual training will weed out 85% of the candidates later. To get this assignment, you have to have very high physical fitness scores and a certain ASVAB score on the academic side. The first thing you do after signing up is go to Navy basic training just like everyone else who enlists. After basic training, you go to SEAL specific pre-BUD/S (Basic Underwater Demolition/SEAL) for a few weeks or even months. Here you will take part in some workouts and paperwork. Eventually you will start school/training, and BUD/S is the first school in the pipeline and is three phases long. BUD/S and the other required training to make up all of SEAL training lasts just over two years.

Something that many people don't consider is that if you enlist to be a Navy SEAL and don't make it through training (and 85% of candidates do not make it through), there is a good chance you will get reassigned to a less desirable job for the rest of your enlistment. You signed up for four years of service and you still owe that time, even if it isn't as a Navy SEAL. The 'cooler' Enlisted jobs get taken by those who were competitively selected, so the only remaining options will be the ones left over that weren't filled initially. Make sure you are picking special ops for the right reasons. Some people are interested because it's the coolest and most elite thing you can do. These are superficial reasons. You need to consider the toll it will take on your future family and your lifestyle. The deployment cycles are a lot more rigorous and challenging than standard positions, and there is no promise you'll even make it home.

To be in Naval special operations on the Officer side, you have to apply for and compete to get a slot in the special warfare community. It is much more selective to get assigned with this as an Officer than it is for Enlisted. At the Naval Academy, roughly 150 midshipmen apply each year and only 12-20 are accepted. After you commission, you get orders to go to BUD/S and take the same courses with the Enlisted members. The attrition rate for BUD/S from the Naval Academy is much lower than it is on the Enlisted side. Only about 20% of the Naval Academy graduates wash out each year. This is because it is so selective to get the assignment that only the cream of the crop get it, and they prepare extensively for BUD/S during their entire four years at the Academy. As a Junior Officer Navy SEAL, you lead your team of SEALs in combat zones. Later in your career when you get senior enough (O3 or O4), you're pulled off the front lines and sit on a forward operations base and direct different units and the joint forces. The Enlisted SEALs will continue as operators and kick down doors almost their entire career.

Special Operators are the badasses of the military and deserve all the credit they get. To succeed and join their ranks, you have to want it more than anything in the world. The trainings are designed to be extremely tough and weed out the people who can't handle the mental grind and the physical pain. You will be broken down and built back up as a team if you make it through. You may be drowned, beaten, kept awake without sleep for days, and pushed to the point that you pass out and physically collapse many times over.

Reserve, National Guard, Merchant Marine

If the active duty lifestyle isn't for you, you could also join the Reserves or the National Guard. Active duty troops work for the military full time and can be deployed overseas at any time. One of the biggest perks of the Reserves and National Guard is not being forced to move every few years to take on a new assignment. This is especially significant to those with children or those with spouses who are tied to a location based on their job or a family member's health. Reserve components fall under each branch of the military, and their purpose is to provide and maintain trained units and personnel to be available for active duty when needed (i.e. in times of war or national emergency). They also fill the gaps in stateside service positions when active duty forces deploy overseas. Members of the Reserve participate in training drills one weekend per month, as well as two weeks per year. They typically also hold a full-time job in the civilian sector. Depending on your

Reserve unit, you may also be able to condense your training time into quarterly or even bi-annual sessions instead of monthly.

National Guard consists of the Army National Guard and the Air Force Air National Guard. It is organized and controlled by state, but in times of war it can be federalized and deployed. They assist during local emergencies and can serve in a variety of roles while deployed overseas. Like the Reserves, they participate in training drills one weekend per month and two weeks per year. Both the Reserve and National Guard can deploy overseas. The current overseas conflicts (Operation Iraqi Freedom, Operation Enduring Freedom, Operation New Dawn) have an all-volunteer force, so as of now you would not be forced to deploy overseas.

The Merchant Marine consists of a fleet of merchant ships operated by either the private sector or the government that engage in commerce or transportation during peacetime. It is an auxiliary of the Navy and can be called to deliver troops and materials in times of war. It is made up of Mariners, not Marines, who are considered civilians unless it is a time of war (in which case they are considered military personnel).

Depending on your status in one of the above organizations, and maybe depending on if you have deployed overseas to a combat zone, you can enjoy some of the military and veteran benefits available. If you are interested in one of these organizations, I encourage you to look into the education opportunities and lifestyles to make sure it is a good fit for you.

What You Sacrifice by Joining the Military

This section is important because you should not make the decision to join the military without realizing the sacrifices it entails. I believe it is absolutely worth it and have no regrets about serving, and I think it would be a good experience for anyone who approaches it with the right mindset. However, it is important to know that the military is not for everyone.

Joining the military requires you to sign a contract and hand your life over to their needs. This is an obligation that you cannot take back. You owe them the time you have signed up for, and they can use you as they see fit. This includes doing the work they need you to do, when they need you to do it, in the location they want you to do it in. Some of your freedoms will be impacted while on active duty. This includes limits on your free speech, following their rules at all times, and being tried under military law if you end up in court (the rules are different in the military). You may even lose your life in the line of duty; it is a sacrifice you need to fully understand and agree to before choosing this path.

The military will force you to move every few years to take on a new assignment, and this can take a toll on families and especially children. It is not much of an issue for someone who is single, but if you find that special someone while still on active duty, there will come a time where he/she either has to move with you to your new assignment or you have to work out a long-distance relationship. As an example, one of my Commanders who stayed in for a full career had been active duty for 24 years and had daughters in high school when he got a new assignment. His daughters and his wife did not want to move again at this time in their lives just for this two-year assignment, so they decided to stay put in their current home and my Commander moved by himself to his new base. He worked there M-F and drove many hours home to see his family on certain weekends. This lasted for a full two years. If you stay in the military long-term, this is a very real possibility at some point.

Deployments are not optional and will take you away from your loved ones and your normal luxuries for an extended period of time. Think of a stereotypical military movie where our troops are living in tents in the middle of the desert; this is kind of like a deployment depending on which base you end up at. Deployments support one of the overseas conflicts and focus on the operational mission. The U.S. has many bases spread throughout the Middle East (as well as Africa and a few countries in other continents). The bases vary widely in size and mission, but imagine a small self-sustaining community dropped in the middle of the desert. While deployed, you will probably work six-day workweeks for 10-12+ hours per day. You will not get vacation, you will not be allowed to travel outside of the base or city, you may not be able to drink alcohol depending on the country you are in – you basically do your job and that's it. But on the bright side, you will get to see our military's war fighting capabilities and enjoy a variety of perks while deployed and when you return (more info on this in the Perks section below).

Loans, Scholarships, & College Expenses

Let's say you want to know what other options there are besides the military paths described in this book. If you aren't one of the lucky few to have your parents pay for your college education, you will have to pay for it through a combination of loans, scholarships, grants, and old-fashioned work. Loans require you to pay them back at some point, and all of them will eventually start charging you interest. If you're able to get grants and independent scholarships, go for it. Grants and scholarships do not have to be repaid. The only issue with grants and scholarships is they are very competitive. If you are a minority or have a unique history, your chances of getting a scholarship are higher. Each grant or scholarship has its own application criteria and its own requirements. Many will ask you to write an essay or answer several questions in detail, and while you may be able to re-use some essays on multiple applications, it is a process that takes a lot of time. There is also no guarantee that you will be successful. When I was applying for scholarships, I spent several hours each on about ten different scholarships I applied for, and I ended up with around $3,500 to show for my efforts. It's better than nothing, but not close to covering the $200,000 I needed for my private-school expenses.

What kind of expenses can you expect for college besides tuition? Books can cost over $1,000 per semester. For some classes you can rent used textbooks online for much cheaper than they cost brand new, but for other classes you have to buy a textbook that is written by the professor and is filled in throughout the class. They update the version each year so you can't buy an old one from a previous student.

Saving money on room & board by living off-campus may not be an option depending on which school you attend. My school required students to live on-campus their first two years and have an on-campus meal plan. Many schools require the first year or two to be on-campus, and some require all four years. A full year of on-campus room & board (which does not include the summer between grades) typically costs $10,000-$15,000.

Besides the above costs, you also need some spending money to pay for things like toiletries, clothes, meals out, entertainment, etc. All of these costs add up. Balancing a part-time job with school is an option, but the more time you spend working, the less time you have to focus on studies. A ROTC scholarship will cover all of the expenses mentioned above, and the monthly stipend allowed me to still have fun without needing a job at all. I was able to balance school with ROTC, campus organizations, and Greek life.

Perks of the Military

Serving in the military comes with many perks while on active duty and after separation (in which case you are called a veteran) or retirement (in which case you are called a retiree). Earlier in this book we touched on the sacrifices you have to make as a member of the military. The following perks are a great return in exchange for the sacrifices you will make.

- One of the most attractive perks of a career in the military is the Retirement pay you will receive once you have served for 20 years. At the 20-year point, you will earn half of your base pay for the rest of your life without having to work for it ever again. For a 38-year-old Master Sergeant who Enlisted at age 18, this would probably mean $29,000 per year (higher if the rank was E8 or E9). For a 42-year-old Lieutenant Colonel who commissioned at age 22, this would probably mean about $50,000 per year. You may also receive some disability pay as compensation for the negative effects your military service had on your body. This could add up to another $3,200 per month for full disability if you have a spouse and child. If you continue serving past the 20-year mark, you will add 2.5% of your base pay for each additional year you served. A 25-year career would earn you 62.5% of your base pay each year, which would be $83,000 per year for a Colonel.

- Based on the location of your assignment, your housing allowance will increase or decrease to align with the local cost of living. The Housing Allowance (BAH) for a new 2nd Lieutenant in the Midwest may be around $1,000 per month, but if you were in Boston or LA, it could be $3,000+ per month instead – which is paid on top of your base pay with additional allowance for food. If you have a spouse and/or children, you also will be paid a bit more to help cover the cost of taking care of them.

- You will earn 2.5 days of leave per month while active duty. This adds up to 30 days per year and rolls over to the next year (to an extent, there is a max amount of leave you can build up per fiscal year). The only downside is if you take a trip and are gone over a weekend, you have to use days of leave for the weekend days you are gone as well. Many military jobs are M-F work weeks and give you the weekend off. Depending on if your job is considered 'mission essential' or not, you can also get all 10 federal holidays off. Many bases will add another day for four or five of those federal holidays to give you a four-day weekend (Memorial Day, 4th of July, Labor Day, Thanksgiving, Christmas), and some bases will also give you extra time off around the Christmas timeframe. When you add it all up, if you were to use all of your vacation days in a year, you would only average 4.016 work days per week. Not bad.

- You do not have to pay federal tax on your base pay for every month you are deployed. This would include the entire departure month if you deployed in the middle or end of the month, and the entire return month if you returned early in a month. On my deployment, this perk saved me about $4,500 based on my pay at the time.

- While deployed, you will continue to receive your Basic Allowance for Housing. If you do not have a family or dependent that needs to stay in your house while you're gone, you can get out of your lease with no penalties, put your belongings in storage, and pocket the $1,000 - $1,500 per month that would normally go towards your rent. This saved me about $8,500 on my deployment, and I lived in the Midwest. A more expensive area could have doubled or tripled this amount.

- The last deployment perk is additional pay you earn based on where you are deployed. Many bases in the Middle East will earn you some combination of hardship duty pay, hazardous duty pay, or imminent danger pay. Other additional pay you could get (separate from a deployment) include assignment incentive pay for taking a new assignment, multiyear retention bonuses for extending your service commitment for several years, or Cost of Living Allowance and overseas housing allowance if you're stationed overseas. I had Enlisted troops who extended their service obligation by six years and earned up to $90,000 cash in return. While at an assignment and depending on your job, you may be asked to travel for your job or brief training, which is called Temporary Duty (TDY). While TDY, you receive money each day called per diem which is used to cover your food expenses, but it is usually much more than you need. You'll also get your travel, hotel and possibly a rental car paid for. On a five-week TDY if you don't spend too much eating out, you can pocket a few thousand dollars from the per diem and mileage earned for driving your private vehicle there instead of flying and renting a car.

- Many credit card companies will waive their annual fee for active duty military and lower your interest rates. A quick google search will reveal fantastic credit cards that normally cost hundreds of dollars each year to use that you can have for free. The perks you will receive can be worth thousands of dollars, and I can personally vouch for that.

- You receive free healthcare, free dental care, and free prescriptions/medications while active duty through TriCare (the military medical insurance company). This benefit also extends to your dependents (spouse & children). You can also expect to receive free healthcare through the VA after separation or retirement based on your disability at the time. This is a very complex system and would take too long to explain in this book, but basically if you receive at least a 10% disability rating upon separation, you can get free healthcare after separation through the VA.

- There are a few vacation websites that offer discounted condos and hotels to military members at participating properties. One of these is the Armed Forces Vacation Club. A few years ago, I went on a trip to the Bahamas with a few friends and got a one-bedroom condo at a resort on the beach for only $350 total for 7 nights. Split with my 2 friends, it was only $120 per person for a week's worth of lodging on a tropical island. If you have an idea of a country or rough area you want to travel to, you will probably be able to find something in that city or region that will save you a lot of money.

- Piggybacking off the above, there are also hotels that are exclusively for military in amazing locations for much cheaper than the market rate. Some of these properties include Hawaii, Orlando, San Diego, and Switzerland.

- You will have the ability to fly space-available, for free, on any military plane that has a seat open. There are many cargo planes that travel across the continental U.S. and overseas that have space for people who need a free ride. It can be a bit of pain because they usually don't post their flight schedule until three days prior to departure. You also begin and end at a military base, and sometimes planes are re-routed at the last minute. If you can work with this, it's a cheap way to fly to Europe or Asia if you have the vacation time.

- You have a retirement fund available to you called the Thrift Savings Plan (TSP), and you can put part of your paycheck into this every month to save up for retirement. Under the new flexible retirement plan, you can also have up to 5% of your contributions matched, which is free money. It is similar to an IRA or 401K, but there are not as many investment options. However, the fees charged for managing this fund are extremely low compared to market rates. And after you separate or retire, you can either leave the money in the funds to continue to accumulate compound interest or you can transfer it to your own IRA or 401K.

- Many airlines allow active duty military to check baggage for free, and some of the airlines who charge for carry-on bags make these free to military as well (such as discount airlines). Also, many airlines allow active duty military to board very early in the boarding process.

- Depending on the city you live in, you can receive perks such as free tickets to baseball games, free public transportation, etc. Each city is different so ask around.

- Many companies, restaurants and retail stores offer discounts to active duty military and veterans. Some I know of include Lowes, Great Clips, Home Depot, Dell, Sam's Club, Apple, Zales, most of the major cell phone plan companies, many hotels, and lots of restaurant chains.

- To piggyback off the above bullet, many businesses offer outstanding deals to the military on Veterans Day each year! On November 11th, you can visit one or several of the many restaurants who participate and get a free or discounted meal. You can hop around for breakfast, lunch and dinner and get a day's worth of food for free (but be sure to tip). Other options besides restaurants include free haircuts and discounts on merchandise at many stores, including a lot of the larger chains. Be sure to support these companies in return for their generosity.

Post-military job options

Once you separate from the military, you're able to pursue whatever you want to! School is an obvious option if you Enlisted and still want to earn a bachelor's degree, or if you already have your degree and want to get a Master's. Another option you may not have considered is working for the Federal Government as a GS (General Schedule) employee and doing a similar job to the one you did as active duty military. Your resume at this point is probably perfect for a transition into the same career field doing close to the same thing. If you don't know much about federal service, it provides extremely high job stability so you don't need to worry about being laid off. Your pay will be based on the job you take and its associated pay grade, and you will earn more either as you work that job longer or if you promote to another job in a higher pay grade. If you accept a job at a different location, many times you can get your move paid for by the government. And there is a retirement program for civil service so you can receive paychecks for the rest of your life after you retire. Another great perk is good work-life balance. Many federal jobs only require 40-hour workweeks with overtime pay for longer workweeks (and it may be optional to work over your limit).

The private sector is the other obvious option. While you will probably have less job stability than in federal service and have a higher chance of longer work hours, you could receive higher pay and better perks like stock options. You're free to pursue whichever path you desire and now have the freedom to leave a job if you don't like it or have a better opportunity elsewhere.

My path

I was able to follow my path because I knew about ROTC scholarships and wanted to spend a portion of my life serving my country. While a senior in high school, I applied for a four-year Air Force

ROTC scholarship and was awarded a Type-II, which back in 2010 paid for up to $18,000 of tuition per year, a books stipend, and a monthly living stipend. That would've covered tuition at almost any public university, but I went to a private school (TCU) and would have had to pay the difference in tuition out of pocket. Lucky for me, TCU is a Yellow Ribbon school that will pay for 100% of the difference in my ROTC scholarship and the normal cost of tuition.

Conclusion

You now have the information you need to make an educated decision on whether one of the paths identified in this book is the right fit for you! Please share this knowledge with friends and family. I wish the entire country knew about the details of these options, even though the military will not be the right fit for everyone.

If you noticed any information you think may be outdated or incorrect, or any typos, I would really appreciate it if you let me know! Many rounds of edits were put into this book but something will always slip through the cracks. Please send comments or feedback to PatrioticPayback@gmail.com. Thanks!

I hope you are able to use the lessons learned from this book to help you figure out your next step in your personal and professional life. Good luck and God bless.

- Mitch

ACKNOWLEDGMENTS

Thank you to my parents for setting me up for success. Thank you to my brothers for their support and their perspective on life at the Service Academies. Thank you to Cecily for making my time in St. Louis so much better. Thank you to 375 CONS and 379 ECONS for a great Air Force experience. And thank you to God for guiding me and giving me the second chance I didn't deserve.

"A man's life is what his thoughts make of it."– Marcus Aurelius

"To know and not to do is really not to know." – Stephen Covey

"Two men look out of prison bars, one sees mud, the other sees stars." – Dale Carnegie

"You're always one decision away from a totally different life."

"If you believe your limits, your life will be very limited."

"Influencing people is the art of letting them have your way." – Chris Voss

Book Suggestions

The Willpower Instinct – Kelly McGonigal

Life, Liberty, and the Pursuit of Entrepreneurship – M.J. DeMarco

How to Win Friends & Influence People – Dale Carnegie

Influence: The Psychology of Persuasion – Robert Cialdini

The 7 Habits of Highly Effective People – Stephen Covey

Think & Grow Rich – Napoleon Hill

Never Split the Difference – Chris Voss

ROTC/G.I. Bill/Academy Resources

https://www.afrotc.com/

https://www.goarmy.com/rotc.html

https://www.nrotc.navy.mil/

https://www.benefits.va.gov/gibill/post911_gibill.asp

https://www.benefits.va.gov/gibill/montgomery_bill.asp

https://www.military.com/education/gi-bill/new-post-911-gi-bill-overview.html

https://www.militarytimes.com/education-transition/2019/07/20/gi-bill-benefits-guide/

https://www.academyadmissions.com/

https://www.usna.edu/Admissions/index.php

https://westpoint.edu/admissions

https://www.uscga.edu/admissions/

https://www.usmma.edu/admissions

Non-Fiction Military Books

Fearless – Eric Blehm

Black Hawk Down – Mark Bowden

Red Platoon: A True Story of American Valor – Clinton Romesha

Band of Brothers – Stephen E. Ambrose

The Art of War – Sun Tzu

D-Day, 1944: Voices from Normandy – Robert Neillands and Roderick De Normann

ABOUT THE AUTHOR

Mitchell grew up in Colleyville, Texas. After being awarded a Type II AFROTC scholarship his senior year of high school, he attended Texas Christian University in Fort Worth, Texas, where he split his time between class, ROTC, and Greek life activities. He majored in Entrepreneurial Management and graduated in May of 2014, and upon commissioning, began his active duty career at Scott Air Force Base in Illinois. In addition to his time spent at Scott AFB, he also participated in a 6-month deployment to the Middle East and a handful of TDYs across the country. Mitchell gathered the knowledge necessary for this book through his ROTC experiences, interviews with his brothers who attended the Air Force Academy and Naval Academy, conversations with the enlisted Airmen in his units, and lots of research. Now a separated Captain, Mitchell has set his sights on a move to Phoenix to soak up the sunshine and pursue his entrepreneurial endeavors.